Wise Old Sayings for Children

Timeless Phrases that Teach Values and Wisdom

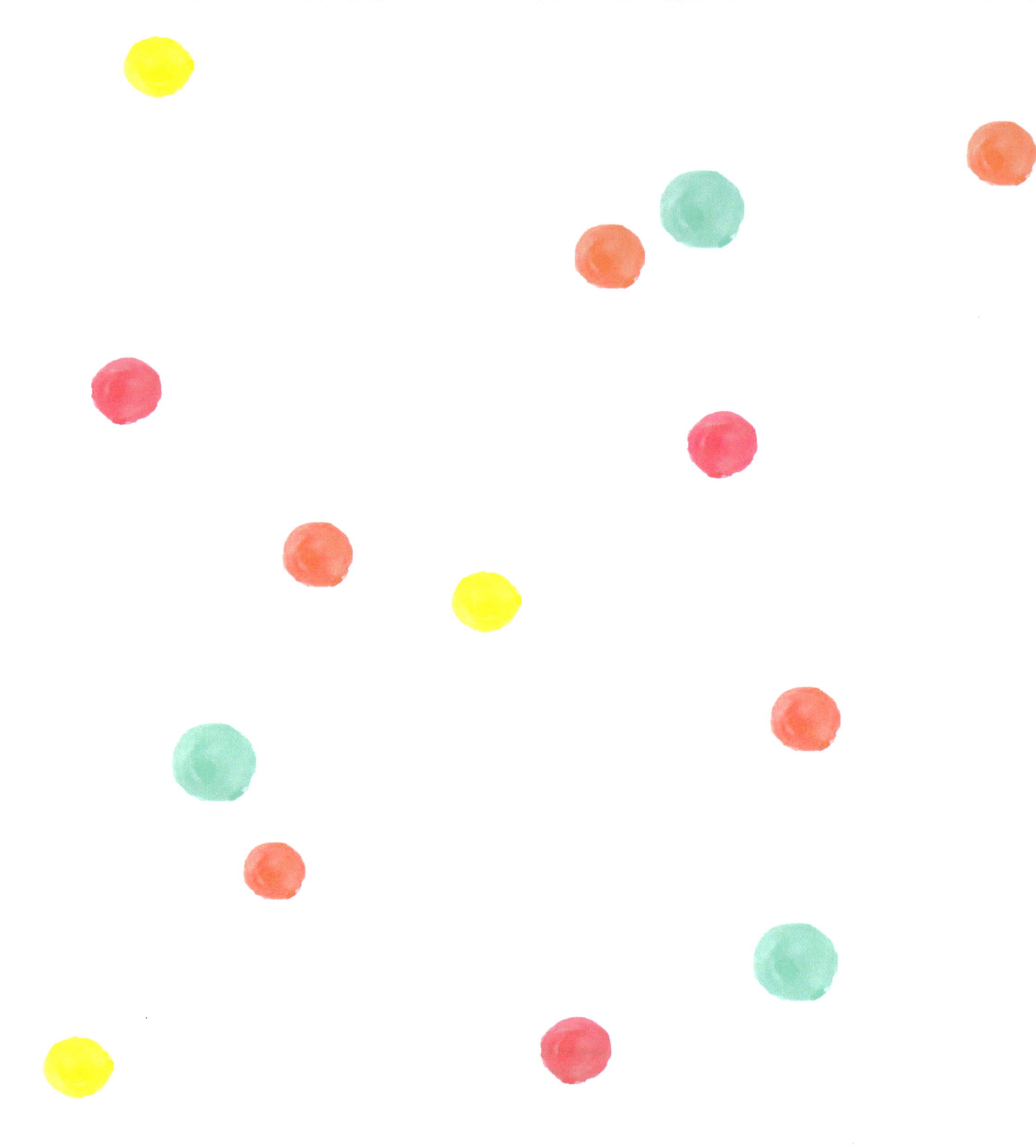

Once upon a time,
we took a look.
We learned so many things
from the pages of
that book!

Table of Contents

- A Stitch in Time Saves Nine — 1
- Early to Bed and Early to Rise — 3
- A Penny Saved is a Penny Earned — 4
- Don't Count Your Chickens Before they Hatch — 5
- There's no use Crying Over Spilled Milk — 7
- The Early Bird Gets the Worm — 9
- A Rolling Stone Gathers no Moss — 11
- All that Glitters is Not Gold — 12
- Great Oaks from Mighty Acorns Grow — 13
- Don't Put All Your Eggs into One Basket — 15
- Look Before You Leap — 16

Hello there my little Sweeties,
I'm Ms. Fairweather.
Find me on each page—
I will help you along.
I will help you to learn how to
grow wise and strong!

An early bedtime will help you to get the new day off to a *great* start!

Early to bed and early to rise, makes a man *healthy*, wealthy, <u>and</u> *wise*.

Dream. Strive. Learn. believe. Grow. But most of all, be yourself!

My darling geniuses!
You've finished— now don't you feel smart?
    I'm so proud of you....
but then again,
    I always have been,
  right from the start.

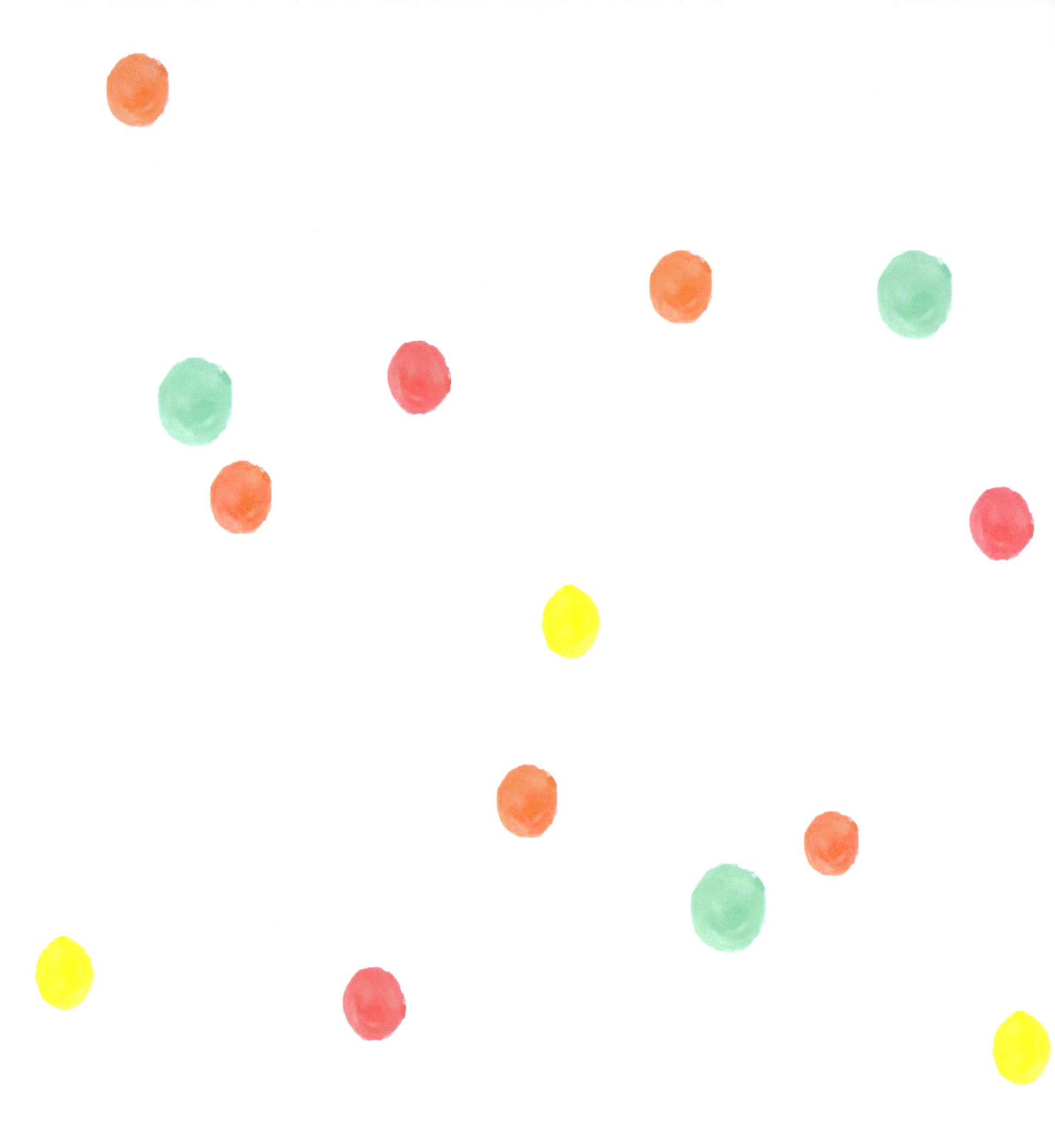

Copyright © 2022 Michael Slabaugh.

All rights reserved. No part of this publication may be reproduced, distributed, or transmitted in any form or by
electronic means, including photocopying, recording, or other electronic or mechanical methods, without the prior written permission of the author, except in the case of
educational or non-commercial purposes permitted by law. For permission requests, write to the permissions coordinator at the address listed below.

ISBN : 979-8-9859180-0-7 (Paperback)

Front cover and illustrations by:
Kristin Jackson and Monica Linford

Text by: Michael Slabaugh and Mary Ann Francis

Printed by: Amazon Kindle Direct Publishing

First printing edition 2022

Imagine L. J. Publishing
2650 Madison Ave.
Ogden, UT 84401